Syria, Iran, and Hezbollah:

the Unholy Alliance and Its War on Lebanon

SYRIA, IRAN, AND HEZBOLLAH:
THE UNHOLY ALLIANCE AND ITS WAR ON LEBANON

Marius Deeb

HOOVER INSTITUTION PRESS
Stanford University   Stanford, California

www.hoover.org

Hoover Institution Press Publication No. 640

Hoover Institution at Leland Stanford Junior University, Stanford, California, 94305-6010

First printing 2013
20 19 18 17 16 15 14 13   9 8 7 6 5 4 3 2

Manufactured in the United States of America

The paper used in this publication meets the minimum Requirements of the American National Standard for Information Sciences—Permanence of Paper for Printed Library Materials, ANSI/NISO Z39.48-1992. ♾

Cataloging-in-Publication Data is available from the Library of Congress.
ISBN 978-0-8179-1665-7 (pbk.: alk. paper)
ISBN 978-0-8179-1666-4 (e-book)
ISBN 978-0-8179-1667-1 (mobi)
ISBN 978-0-8179-1668-8 (pdf)

*The Hoover Institution gratefully acknowledges
the following individuals and foundations
for their significant support of the*

HERBERT AND JANE DWIGHT WORKING GROUP
ON ISLAMISM AND THE INTERNATIONAL ORDER:

Herbert and Jane Dwight

Beall Family Foundation

Stephen Bechtel Foundation

Lynde and Harry Bradley Foundation

Mr. and Mrs. Clayton W. Frye Jr.

Lakeside Foundation

Contents

CONTENTS

FOREWORD

FOR DECADES, the themes of the Hoover Institution have revolved around the broad concerns of political and economic and individual freedom. The Cold War that engaged and challenged our nation during the twentieth century guided a good deal of Hoover's work, including its archival accumulation and research studies. The steady output of work on the communist world offers durable testimonies to that time, and struggle. But there is no repose from history's exertions, and no sooner had communism left the stage of history than a huge challenge arose in the broad lands of the Islamic world. A brief respite, and a meandering road, led from the fall of the Berlin Wall on 11/9 in 1989 to 9/11. Hoover's project, the Herbert and Jane Dwight Working Group on Islamism and the International Order, is our contribution to a deeper understanding of the struggle in the Islamic world between order and its nemesis, between Muslims keen to protect the rule of reason and the gains of modernity, and those determined to deny the Islamic world its place in the modern international order of states. The United States is deeply engaged, and dangerously exposed, in the Islamic world, and we see our working group as part and parcel of the ongoing confrontation with the radical Islamists who have declared war on the states in their midst, on American power and interests, and on the very order of the international state system.

The Islamists are doubtless a minority in the world of Islam. But they are a determined breed. Their world is the Islamic emirate, led by self-styled "emirs and mujahedeen in the path of God" and legitimized by the pursuit of the caliphate that collapsed with the end of the Ottoman Empire in 1924. These masters of terror and their foot soldiers have made it increasingly difficult to integrate the world of Islam into modernity. In the best of worlds, the entry of Muslims into modern culture and economics would have presented difficulties of no small consequence: the strictures on women, the legacy of humiliation and self-pity, the outdated educational systems, and an explosive demography that is forever at war with social and economic gains. But the borders these warriors of the faith have erected between Islam and "the other" are particularly forbidding. The lands of Islam were the lands of a crossroads civilization, trading routes and mixed populations. The Islamists have waged war, and a brutally effective one it has to be conceded, against that civilizational inheritance. The leap into the modern world economy as attained by China and India in recent years will be virtually impossible in a culture that feeds off belligerent self-pity, and endlessly calls for wars of faith.

The war of ideas with radical Islamism is inescapably central to this Hoover endeavor. The strategic context of this clash, the landscape of that Greater Middle East, is the other pillar. We face three layers of danger in the heartland of the Islamic world: states that have succumbed to the sway of terrorists in which state authority no longer exists (Afghanistan, Somalia, and Yemen), dictatorial regimes that suppress their people at home and pursue deadly weapons of mass destruction and adventurism abroad (Iraq under Saddam Hussein, the Iranian theocracy), and "enabler" regimes, such as the ones in Egypt and Saudi Arabia, which export their own problems with radical Islamism to other parts of the Islamic world and beyond. In this context, the task of reversing Islamist radicalism and of reforming and strengthening the state across the entire Muslim world—the Middle East, Africa, as well as South, Southeast, and Central Asia—is the greatest strategic challenge of the twenty-first century. The essential starting point is detailed knowledge of our enemy.

Thus, the working group will draw on the intellectual resources of Hoover and Stanford and on an array of scholars and practitioners from elsewhere in the United States from the Middle East and the broader world of Islam. The scholarship on contemporary Islam can now be read with discernment. A good deal of it, produced in the immediate aftermath of 9/11, was not particularly deep and did not stand the test of time and events. We, however, are in the favorable position of a "second generation" assessment of that Islamic material. Our scholars and experts can report, in a detailed, authoritative way, on Islam within the Arabian Peninsula, on trends within Egyptian Islam, on the struggle between the Kemalist secular tradition in Turkey and the new Islamists, particularly the fight for the loyalty of European Islam between those who accept the canon, and the discipline, of modernism and those who do not.

Arabs and Muslims need not be believers in American exceptionalism, but our hope is to engage them in this contest of ideas. We will not necessarily aim at producing primary scholarship, but such scholarship may materialize in that our participants are researchers who know their subjects intimately. We see our critical output as essays accessible to a broader audience, primers about matters that require explication, op-eds, writings that will become part of the public debate, and short, engaging books that can illuminate the choices and the struggles in modern Islam.

We see this endeavor as a faithful reflection of the values that animate a decent, moderate society. We know the travails of modern Islam, and this working group will be unsparing in depicting them. But we also know that the battle for modern Islam is not yet lost, that there are brave men and women fighting to retrieve their faith from the extremists. Some of our participants will themselves be intellectuals and public figures who have stood up to the pressure. The working group will be unapologetic about America's role in the Muslim world. A power that laid to waste religious tyranny in Afghanistan and despotism in Iraq, that came to the rescue of the Muslims in the Balkans when they appeared all but doomed, has given much to those burdened populations. We haven't always understood Islam and Muslims—hence this inquiry. But it is a given of the working group that the pursuit of modernity and human welfare, and of the rule of law and reason, in Islamic lands is the common ground between America and contemporary Islam.

LEBANESE DON'T HAVE TO BE unduly old or nostalgic to recall a different, and a better country. The sects, all eighteen of them, jostled and quarreled, but their feuds were child's play when compared to the hell and the disorder they would come to know. The place had its pretensions: there were Lebanese who thought of their country as a piece of Europe at the foot of a splendid mountain. There were communities and neighborhoods that mimicked the ways, and savored the language of France, the power that had marked out the boundaries of modern Lebanon, in 1920. There were Arab nationalists who dismissed all that and looked eastward, toward Syria, and the bigger Arab world beyond. There was even a neighborhood, on the bay of Beirut, made in the American image, shaped by the American University of Beirut that the Protestant missionaries had founded in the 1860s. The creed of the place tolerated and jumbled all these conceptions of Lebanon.

Nowadays, a different order prevails in the country, if order can be ascribed to Lebanon. The border that had separated Lebanon from Syria, its eastern neighbor, was all but erased by a dictatorship in Damascus bent on the conquest of Lebanon. There came a time, in the 1990s, when the Syrians emptied Lebanon of any meaningful shred of sovereignty. Critics of

Syria, political and religious leaders, journalists and men and women of letters, were struck down with frequency. Western power had retreated from Lebanon, and the Syrians had turned that country into a vassal state. The Iranian theocracy was to follow: Eager to establish a beachhead on the Mediterranean, a sister republic, if you will, the Iranians bought and subverted their way into the vulnerable country. A militant group, Hezbollah, armed, financed, and wholly owned by the Iranian rulers, was to become a state within a state, with a military arsenal that put to shame the resources of the national army, with vast financial resources provided it by Iran and by criminal rackets of every kind. It would be true to say that the Lebanese no longer recognized the country of their memory and national narrative.

We are indeed lucky to have this outstanding work by the historian Marius Deeb. A child of Lebanon, he was formed by its open, Levantine culture. Steeped in the history and literary heritage of Lebanon, he has both described the new order of Lebanon, and summoned a nobler history. Professor Deeb knows intimately that haunting country. The son of a noted educator in Beirut, he grew up in that city, and he knew as well the world of the southern hinterland where his ancestral village is located. Marius Deeb came into his own in the most modern and vibrant enclave of Beirut, the American enclave, at a time when young men and women read books and pamphlets, took in the modern world, and were confident that a better future beckoned.

FOUAD AJAMI
Senior Fellow, Hoover Institution—
Co-chairman, Herbert and Jane Dwight Working Group
on Islamism and the International Order

Syria, Iran, and Hezbollah:

the Unholy Alliance and Its War on Lebanon

MARIUS DEEB

INTRODUCTION

Pᴿᴱˢᴵᴰᴱᴺᵀ Hᴀꜰᴇᴢ ᴀʟ-Aˢˢᴀᴅ had allied Syria with Iran soon after the triumph of Ayatollah Khomeini's Islamic Revolution in Iran. There were three major reasons for this alliance. First, being an Alawite, Assad sought an alliance with Shi'ite Iran because the Sunnis had persecuted the Alawites since medieval times. From the mid-1970s onwards, the Syrian ruler was challenged by a militant Sunni movement, the Muslim Brotherhood: An alliance with an Islamic Iran whose ideology was anti-Western and anti-Israeli would help him domestically and regionally. Second, the Islamic Revolution

1

could be used to mobilize the Shi'ite community in Lebanon and render it an ally of the Alawi-controlled regime in Syria. Third, the methods used by the new Islamic Iran, that is, terrorism in general and the suicide bomber in particular, would make Iran an ideal ally of Assad who had, since 1975, used terrorism to achieve his goals of dominating Lebanon and undermining the peace process between Israel and the Arab countries.

The establishment of Hezbollah by Iran and Syria in June 1982 as a joint venture was indicative of the strong alliance that cemented these two countries. Hezbollah was created to be the terrorist organization par excellence serving its two masters, Iran and Syria.

When Hezbollah came to being, Israel had just begun its military campaign known as "Peace for Galilee" to liberate Lebanon from the Palestine Liberation Organization (PLO), and this was done in alliance with the young charismatic Christian leader Bachir Gemayel. The latter, who was elected president of Lebanon on August 23, 1982, wanted to liberate Lebanon from both the PLO and Syrian occupation, so an agent of the Assad regime assassinated Gemayel on September 14, 1982. This was followed by the massacre of unarmed civilians in the Palestinian refugee camps of Sabra and Shatila. This led to the return to Beirut of the Multinational Forces (MNF), composed of American, French, Italian, and British forces that were originally deployed for the evacuation of the PLO fighters in early September 1982.

Lebanon was occupied by Syria by the end of 1976, but the Israeli military campaign of 1982 pushed the Syrian army out of more than half of the Lebanese territories, including Beirut. The U.S. sponsored direct negotiations between the Israeli and Lebanese governments to negotiate a quasi peace treaty that would pacify permanently the Lebanese-Israeli border. This was anathema to Assad, who wanted to keep the Lebanese-Israeli border ablaze so that he could continue fighting Israel through his proxy militias and terrorist groups. He could not do the same through the Syrian-Israeli border, as it had been sealed off since the signing with Israel of the Syria-Israel Disengagement Agreement on May 31, 1974. Hezbollah was created precisely to push the MNF out of Lebanon, to prevent any peace accord between Lebanon and Israel, and to make it possible for Assad to impose his dominion over Lebanon once again.

TERRORISM AND HOSTAGE TAKING

The first terrorist operation by Hezbollah directed against the United States was the bombing of the American Embassy in Beirut on April 18, 1983, that killed 49 people and wounded over a hundred. This was followed by the simultaneous suicide bombing of the American and French contingents of the MNF on October 23, 1983, that killed 241 U.S. Marines and wounded 70 others, as well as killing 58 French soldiers and wounding 15 others. The president of the American University of Beirut, Malcolm Kerr, a distinguished Arabist born in Lebanon to a family of American educators dedicated to the welfare of the region, was assassinated on campus by Hezbollah on January 18, 1984. President Amine Gemayel, who was elected in September 1982 succeeding his assassinated brother Bachir, came under tremendous pressure from President Assad, who used Shi'ite and Druze militias to abrogate the Lebanese-Israeli Accord signed on May 17, 1983. As a consequence of the military and terrorist campaign pursued by Syria, the MNF evacuated Lebanon by the end of March 1984. The Lebanese government canceled the Lebanese-Israeli Accord on March 5, 1984, and the campaign of taking American and French nationals as hostages commenced with the kidnapping of the CIA bureau chief in Beirut, William Buckley, on March 16, 1984, who was tortured and killed. Other major terrorist operations against the United States by Hezbollah working for Syria and Iran included the suicide bombing of the U.S. Embassy annex on September 20, 1984, killing twenty-three people and wounding sixteen others. And second was the kidnapping of the U.S. observer with the United Nations in southern Lebanon, Lieutenant Colonel William Higgins, on February 17, 1988, who was murdered in July 1989. The hostage taking continued for over seven years, ending with the release of the last hostage, Terry Anderson, on December 4, 1991. Hezbollah was the major organization used by Syria and Iran to take hostages, killing or releasing them as Syria and Iran deemed necessary. Taking hostages and the terrorism directed against France and the United States prevented Gemayel from getting any help from the international community to withstand Syria's terrorist war on Lebanon.

An interim prime minister, Michel Aoun, the commander of Lebanon's army, who was appointed to succeed President Amine Gemayel in September 1988, declared a war of liberation from Syrian domination on March 14, 1989. Aoun had overwhelming support among the Lebanese people and support from some major Arab countries and France, but the United States needed President Assad as an ally against Saddam Hussein in the first Gulf War and gave a green light to Syria to mount a military campaign to dislodge Aoun from the Lebanese presidential palace on October 13, 1990. Thus Lebanon came under total Syrian domination and lost its independence and sovereignty for the next fifteen years.

In the aftermath of the Gulf War of 1991, Assad had no choice but to join the peace process that involved negotiations with Israel under the auspices of the United States. As discussed in my work *Syria's Terrorist War on Lebanon and the Peace Process* (see bibliographical essay at the end), Syria had no intention of making peace with Israel, and Hezbollah was ever ready to provoke a war with Israel whenever the Israeli negotiators became more forthcoming in their quest for peace with Syria. This was the case in July 1993 when Israel launched its Operation Accountability, and again in April 1996 when it mounted a military campaign called "The Grapes of Wrath." In both cases, Hezbollah acted on behalf of Syria and Iran to provoke these wars so that Israel would appear to be making war and not seeking peace. Two major terrorist operations were perpetrated during the same period by the Syria-Iran-Hezbollah axis and were related to what was happening in Lebanon and the peace process. Allegedly in retaliation for the killing of the leader of Hezbollah, Abbas al-Musawi, on February 16, 1992, a terrorist operation destroyed the Israeli Embassy in Buenos Aires on March 17, 1992, resulting in the death of 20 people and the wounding of 240. When Shimon Peres claimed that Israel had a

7

long arm, the spiritual leader of Hezbollah, Mohammad Hussein Fadlallah, proudly retorted: "I thought our holy fighters have already taught him whose arm is longer when they reached the Israelis in Argentina." When Israel kidnapped a top security Hezbollah officer, Mustafa Dirani, on May 21, 1994, the deputy secretary general of Hezbollah threatened that "the strongest blow ever will be dealt to the enemy [Israel] soon." On July 18, 1994, a suicide bomber targeted the building of the Argentine-Israeli Mutual Association in Buenos Aires, killing some 100 people and wounding 230.

When Israel decided to dismantle its security zone in southern Lebanon in May 2000, President Assad panicked because this meant that there was no longer any reason for Hezbollah to continue to fight Israel across the Lebanese-Israeli border. The Syrian president contrived a pretext for Hezbollah by claiming that a small piece of land called Shib'a Farms, which is part of the Golan Heights, is Lebanese territory. Ironically, the Israeli withdrawal from the security zone that neither Hezbollah nor its Syrian master wanted became a day for celebrating the

"Liberation of Lebanon" from Israeli occupation. In reality, Hezbollah and its Syrian master had delayed the Israeli withdrawal from Lebanon for seventeen years, and all the death and destruction brought about by the conflicts and wars that Hezbollah provoked were contrived and unnecessary.

PATRIARCH SFAIR: THE CONSCIENCE OF LEBANON

In the aftermath of the Israeli withdrawal from southern Lebanon in May 2000, and the death of Syrian President Hafez al-Assad in June 2000, the Maronite Catholic Church, in the person of its Patriarch Sfair, issued a memorandum on September 20, 2000, about the suffering of the Lebanese people and, in particular, the Christians under Syrian domination. Sfair pointed out that parliamentary elections since 1992 had been rigged and most elected deputies did not represent the will of the Lebanese people. Syria had selected the members of the Lebanese cabinet, the top civil servants, and even members of the judiciary. The Syrian occupiers were violating the terms of the National Pact of 1943 that affirms: "Neither East nor West, that is, neither France would stay in Lebanon, nor Syria would stay in Lebanon." According to Patriarch Sfair, Lebanon should regain its independence and sovereignty by ending Syrian occupation. Sfair's message found immediate resonance among the Christian communities, and a group of twenty-nine prominent politicians and intellectuals met on April 30, 2001, in the town of Qornet Shehwan, the seat of the Maronite Catholic Bishop of Mount Lebanon, and issued a statement in support of the ideas that Sfair had expressed in his memorandum. This declaration set the stage for the momentous event that happened four years later, that is, the Cedar Revolution.

In early August 2001, Patriarch Sfair embarked on a journey to the southern part of Mount Lebanon, visiting the regions of al-Shouf and Jizzin and, on the way back, the region of Aley. The aim of this journey was the reconciliation between the two religious communities, the Maronites and the Druze, who founded Lebanon in the early eighteenth century. In this journey of uniting the Maronite and Druze communities, Patriarch Sfair was in effect re-founding Lebanon based on its historical roots. An enthusiastic welcome had greeted Patriarch Sfair as he traveled through the towns and villages of these regions. Throngs of people received him, accompanied with music, dancing, and fireworks. In both Christian and Druze villages, roses were strewn and rice was thrown on his path. Statements of welcome and praise of Sfair's mission of "unity and love" were written on various placards that were displayed on the roads leading to the towns and villages that he had visited. One placard read, "The glory of Lebanon has been given to him." Another placard read, "Welcome to the Conscience of Lebanon." Patriarch Sfair visited Deir el Qamar, Mount Lebanon's principal town, where he presided over a mass in the town's cathedral and visited al-Mukhtara, the seat of the feudal Druze leader Walid Jumblatt, where a huge crowd of almost 20 thousand people turned out to greet him. Jumblatt welcomed the patriarch and declared that "the war in Mount Lebanon has gone and will never return;

together we shall protect Mount Lebanon and together we shall protect Lebanon."

The immediate reaction to this successful journey by Patriarch Sfair was the arrest of many supporters of the two leading Christian political movements: the Free National Current, led by General Michel Aoun (exiled from 1990 until 2005); and the Lebanese Forces Party, led by Samir Geagea (imprisoned from 1994 until 2005). These arrests were completely unjustified, leading to a convening of a congress, on August 16, 2001, by political parties and movements, trade unions, and professional organizations covering the spectrum of ideologies in what the five hundred participants called "In Defense of Liberties and Democracy." Although the participants included many Christians and Druze, including Amine Gemayel and Walid Jumblatt, and members of the Qornet Shehwan Gathering, it also had prominent Sunnis and Shi'ites belonging to the political and professional elite, including supporters of Prime Minister Rafic Hariri, the preeminent political figure among the Sunnis.

THE ANTI-SYRIAN OPPOSITION MOVEMENT
GATHERS STRENGTH

As more Lebanese leaders felt stronger in challenging Syrian domination, the chances of using Syria's favorite weapon, terrorism, increased. As early as April 2003, the Lebanese journalist Fares Khashan, who had been close to Prime Minister Hariri, was warned by a well-informed top security official that if the prime minister continues to be at loggerheads with Syrian officials, especially on the issue of extending the term of the incumbent Lebanese president, Émile Lahoud, "he will be assassinated by a suicide bomber." Khashan passed this information to the prime minister immediately after the TV station al-Mustaqbal, which was owned by Hariri, was destroyed in a rocket attack on June 14, 2003. Consequently, Hariri met the Syrian president, who was accompanied by the head of Syrian intelligence in Lebanon, Rustum Ghazaleh, and his predecessor, Ghazi Kanaan. The Syrian message to Hariri was clear: he should exert all his efforts to stop the media campaign against the extension of the term of Lebanese President Lahoud, try to change the policies advocated by the prestigious *al-Nahar* newspaper, stop sending messengers to Patriarch Sfair, stop receiving members of the Christian Qornet Shehwan Gathering, and cease "conspiring" with the Druze leader Walid Jumblatt.

The campaign to prevent the amendment to the Lebanese constitution to make it possible for Lahoud to have an extension of three years for his term in office became the rallying focus for the anti-Syrian opposition. Two important actions taken by France and the United States had empowered the anti-Syrian opposition. First was President George W. Bush signing into law the bill passed by the Congress, "The Syria Accountability and the Lebanese Sovereignty Restoration Act," on December 12, 2003. Second was the landmark UN Security Council Resolution 1559, sponsored by the United States and France, passing on September 2, 2004. The resolution called for free presidential elections, the withdrawal of foreign troops from Lebanon, and the disarming of militias.

Rafic Hariri was summoned to Damascus, where he met President Bashar Assad on August 26, 2004. The meeting lasted less than fifteen minutes, during which the Syrian ruler told him that a vote for the extension of Lahoud's term as president is like voting for Assad. Then he threatened that if Hariri thinks that, in cooperation with French President Jacques Chirac, he could push Syria out, he "will break Lebanon on his head." Hariri eventually decided to vote for the amendment of the Lebanese constitution, which led to the extension, on September 3, 2004, of President Lahoud's term for three years. His reasoning was that it was better to have the incumbent president for three more years than a new president of Lebanon chosen by Syria with the full term of six years. This was insufficient for Assad, for he wanted Hariri to stop coordinating with the Druze leader Walid Jumblatt, with the Christian Qornet Shehwan Gathering, and with Patriarch Sfair. On October 1, 2004, the former minister, Marwan Hamadeh, who was close to Jumblatt, was a target of an unsuccessful assassination attack. Prime Minister Hariri decided to resign on October 21, 2004, and all attempts by Syria to persuade him to stay in power failed. This was an ominous sign. There was a precedent when the Lebanese Prime Minister Rashid Karami, a political figure of great prestige and authority, resigned on May 4, 1987, and refused to go back on his resignation despite Syrian pressure to do so. On June 1, 1987, a bomb killed Karami while he was traveling on a military helicopter.

Hariri, as former prime minister, continued to campaign for the parliamentary elections, publicly stating that with his allies all over Lebanon he would win the elections and form a cabinet that would ask Syria to withdraw its troops from Lebanon in accordance with UN Security Council Resolution 1559. Hariri had made these statements openly, whether by addressing representatives of leading families in Beirut or talking to journalists and politicians at a favored café of his in downtown Beirut. On the same day, February 10, 2005, President Jacques Chirac contacted him with an urgent warning that he should leave Lebanon immediately, as he was in danger. Although Hariri was fully aware of being a target of assassination by the Syrians, he wanted to continue to campaign in Lebanon because he felt that he owed an obligation to his country. He believed that a statesman should campaign in person and not from afar, that is, not from Paris. Hariri was at times naïve when he met periodically and covertly with the leader of Hezbollah, Hassan Nasrallah, hoping to reach an understanding with him during the parliamentary elections and in its aftermath, while Hezbollah was collaborating with Syria in plotting the terrorist operation that would kill Hariri.

The leaders of the Syria-Iran-Hezbollah axis have always believed that by using force and assassinations they can achieve their objectives. There were numerous terrorist operations against leading politicians, journalists, and clergymen in Lebanon and there was no response by the Lebanese people. Those who plotted the assassination of Hariri did not expect any lasting reaction. Over the preceding quarter-century, Lebanese leaders of every stripe had been struck down, and the edifice of Syrian power had held. This time around, it was different. On February 14, 2005, a suicide bomber targeted Hariri's motorcade close to the historic St. George's Hotel on the seafront in Beirut, killing Hariri and twenty-two others. After Hariri's funeral, "it was the Christians and the Druze . . . who daily kept the flame of outrage alive." It took almost a month of daily anti-Syrian protests "for the Sunni community to go into the streets." This culminated in the massive demonstrations of 1.5 million protesters on March 14, 2005, ushering in what is known as the Cedar Revolution.

THE CEDAR REVOLUTION

When 1.5 million people peacefully demonstrated in Beirut on March 14, 2005—calling for the withdrawal of Syrian troops, for a free and democratic polity, and for the truth about the assassination of Hariri and all the other terrorist operations for the last three decades—an unprecedented phenomenon was born, heralding a new era for Lebanon and elsewhere in the region. The Cedar Revolution is the most important event that has taken place in the Middle East since the triumph of the Islamic Revolution in Iran in

February 1979. Unlike the Iranian Revolution that demonized America, reinvented the suicide bomber, and opened the floodgates of terrorism, the Cedar Revolution was a nonviolent revolution with strong adherence to democratic principles and political pluralism, seeking the support of the West and emerging as an antidote to militant Islam and terrorism.

The first achievement of the Cedar Revolution was the withdrawal of the Syrian army and its overt intelligence apparatus from Lebanon on April 26, 2005. The pressure that was exerted by the United States was crucial in achieving this goal.

The unity of the various political parties and movements that the Cedar Revolution was composed of manifested itself on May 4, 2005, when a mass rally was held in Riyad al-Sulh Square in downtown Beirut. It called for the release of Samir Geagea, the leader of the Lebanese Forces Party, who had been incarcerated for eleven years. The speakers at the rally were representative of the political and religious diversity (Christians, Druze, Sunnis, and Shi'ites) of the leaders and followers of the Cedar Revolution. The charismatic leader Michel Aoun returned to

Lebanon on May 7, 2005, after fifteen years in exile, and he was received with tremendous popular enthusiasm. On May 18, 2005, Aoun visited Geagea in his cell at the Ministry of Defense. The hour-long meeting was depicted as "spiritual and emotional," during which they discussed the philosophical and religious books that Geagea had read. Aoun expressed his admiration for Geagea's courage and his "spiritual strength." He added that keeping Geagea in prison was unjust and that he should be released. This was a high point of the Cedar Revolution as the two most popular Christian leaders, who had previously fought a war in 1990, had at last reconciled. Geagea should have responded to Aoun's grand gesture by allying his Lebanese Forces Party to Aoun's Free National Current in the forthcoming parliamentary elections, and by endorsing Aoun for the presidency of Lebanon, but he did not. Unfortunately for the Cedar Revolution, the popularity of Aoun among the Christians and others led the Druze leader Walid Jumblatt and the young Sunni leader, his father's hier, Saad Hariri, to ally themselves in the parliamentary elections with the strongly pro-Syrian Hezbollah and Nabih Berri's Shi'ite Amal Movement. Michel Aoun's popularity conjured up in Walid Jumblatt's mind the image of the Maronite leader Camille Chamoun, who was a formidable rival of the Jumblatt clan in the parliamentary elections in Mount Lebanon during the period of free elections from 1960 until 1972. Hariri's proclivity for dominance prevented him from allying himself with Aoun. Much later, however, Hariri admitted that he had made a mistake by not keeping Aoun within the ranks of the March 14 Movement, that is, the Cedar Revolution. Hariri stated in November 2007: "It [was] possible [then] for Michel Aoun to play a role of bringing the Lebanese together, and be a father to all the groups of March 14." All the leaders of the Cedar Revolution, like Samir Geagea, former president Amine Gemayel, Walid Jumblatt, and Saad Hariri, should have endorsed Michel Aoun for the presidency of Lebanon, for he had earned it by being the pioneer in fighting Syria with his War of Liberation (1989–1990) and by playing a crucial role in the events that led to the Cedar Revolution. By alienating Aoun, the leaders of the Cedar

21

Revolution weakened their position in their struggle against the alliance of Syria, Iran, and Hezbollah.

The parliamentary elections of May–June 2005 were basically fair and free but not up to the standard of the last free elections in Lebanon in 1972. This was because the regions controlled by the fully armed pro-Syrian and pro-Iranian Hezbollah and Amal, southern Lebanon and northern Biqa', candidates who ran against them had been prevented from campaigning by using force or the threat of force. Hezbollah and Amal had made these regions devoid of the freedom to organize politically and, consequently, the results of the elections did not reflect the opinions of their inhabitants.

The results of the parliamentary elections led to the victory of the Cedar Revolution coalition, with 71 deputies out of 128. The new cabinet formed by Fouad Siniora, a Sunni technocrat and trusted aide of the Hariri family, did not include representatives from Michel Aoun's bloc of 27 deputies, but it had to include representatives of Amal and Hezbollah because they had virtually monopolized the representation of the

Shi'ites in parliament. Thus the triumph of the Cedar Revolution was not complete, as it had excluded the large parliamentary bloc led by Aoun (who would eventually be pushed into the arms of Hezbollah) and it had to include Amal and Hezbollah, who were tantamount to a Syrian Trojan horse within the cabinet of the pro-Western and moderate Prime Minister Fouad Siniora.

THE UNHOLY ALLIANCE VERSUS THE CEDAR REVOLUTION

From the outset, the Cedar Revolution had represented, and still represents, the antithesis of the alliance of Syria, Iran, and Hezbollah. In July 2007, the Druze leader Walid Jumblatt organized a gathering supported by all the leaders of the Cedar Revolution. The participants in the gathering called themselves "Those Who Love Life" (Muhibbu al-Hayat). The basic idea was that the struggle between the Cedar Revolution and the alliance of Syria, Iran, and Hezbollah is a clash between two cultures. The Cedar Revolution represents the culture of life. The followers

23

of the Cedar Revolution strongly believe in an independent and free Lebanon. They seek "to struggle for the culture of life, to regain the Lebanese polity as a real homeland . . . for a Lebanese state which is democratic, pluralistic, and a state of law and rights." They also call for "the culture of peace."

The enemies of the Cedar Revolution, like Hezbollah, espouse "the culture of death." Instead of wanting freedom and independence for Lebanon, Hezbollah espouses subservience to its two masters, Syria and Iran. Hezbollah does not tolerate dissent and accuses its critics of treason. Espousing the philosophy of death entails that others who differ with you are threatened, and more often than not threats lead to their demise. Hezbollah's ally, the Amal Movement, led by Speaker of Parliament Nabih Berri, shares the same philosophy of death. When Walid Eido, a member of the Cedar Revolution parliamentary majority, was assassinated on June 13, 2007, his death was reported on the TV network NBN, which is owned and run by Berri. NBN's anchorwoman reported Eido's death with joy and laughter, adding that Eido's assassination was long overdue. She also expressed her wish that the cabinet minister Muhammad Fatfat will be next, wishing him dead too.

Soon after the triumph of the Cedar Revolution, the operatives of Syria, Iran, and Hezbollah began the campaign to eliminate their critics, concentrating on those mass-media figures who had played a major role in the Cedar Revolution. Their first grim deed was the assassination of Samir Kassir, an intellectual, academician, and journalist whose writings in the *al-Nahar* newspaper and his activities were instrumental in mobilizing the rank and file of the Cedar Revolution. May Chidiac, a leading television news personality, survived an assassination attempt on September 25, 2005. This culminated in the assassination of Gebran Tueni on December 12, 2005. He was a leading member of the Cedar Revolution majority in parliament and a longtime critic of Syria and Hezbollah. He was the publisher of the most prestigious newspaper in the Arab world, *al-Nahar*, and his writings inspired supporters of the Cedar Revolution. It was reported that supporters of Hezbollah distributed sweets to celebrate his demise. In a demonstration organized by Hezbollah and its allies against the American Embassy in Beirut, on January 16, 2006, demonstrators chanted repeatedly "Mabruk li-Gebran" (Congratulations to Gebran), expressing their joy over his death. The assassination of Tueni had convinced Walid Jumblatt that Hezbollah cannot be trusted, because it will always remain a proxy of the Iranian-Syrian axis and it will continue to silence those who cherish freedom.

HEZBOLLAH PROVOKES A WAR WITH ISRAEL: JULY 12–AUGUST 14, 2006

The leader of Hezbollah, the Shi'ite cleric Hassan Nasrallah, was asked by the governor of the Lebanese Central Bank to refrain from any action in the summer of 2006 because it was projected to be the best tourist season since the summer of 1974, with an estimated gross gain for the Lebanese economy of $2.5 billion. In an interview with the Kuwaiti newspaper *al-Watan*, Saad Hariri stated that he had discussed the situation in Gaza with Nasrallah five days before the latter launched his operation on July 12, 2006, and clearly depicted the kidnapping of the Israeli soldier by Hamas on June 25, 2006, as a blunder. Hariri had warned that any attempt to kidnap Israeli soldiers, as Hezbollah had tried and failed on May 31, 2006, would result in a devastating war. The kidnapping of two Israeli soldiers by Hezbollah on July 12, 2006, was done to provoke a war with Israel. Syria, Iran, and Hezbollah wanted to turn the tables on the leaders of the Cedar Revolution. To counter the ideals of the Cedar Revolution of nonviolence, liberal democracy, and peace, Hezbollah provoked the war with Israel in the summer of 2006 to subject Lebanon to violence and destruction. During that war, the leader of Hezbollah, Hassan Nasrallah stated that he was going to have an open war with Israel, "whether the Lebanese wanted it or not." The Druze leader Walid Jumblatt pointed out the implicit arrogance of Nasrallah conveyed by this statement. The statement runs contrary to what democracy is all about, where the opinions of the people should prevail.

The war between Hezbollah and Israel ended with the acceptance of United Nations Security

Resolution 1701 on August 14, 2006. The new resolution called for the expansion of the already-existing United Nations Interim Force in Lebanon (UNIFIL) of up to 15,000 troops and for the deployment as well of 15,000 troops of the Lebanese army, and that both forces would be sent to the region that extends from the blue line demarcating the Lebanese-Israeli border to the Litani River. The Lebanese army would confiscate arms found in this region. The army had not been deployed on the border with Israel since 1968. The most important consequence of Hezbollah's war with Israel was that it made Hezbollah lose its raison d'être, that is, to fight Israel across the Lebanese-Israeli border. Despite the destruction that Lebanon suffered and the death of over one thousand Lebanese, Nasrallah, in his speech on September 22, 2006, called the war "a divine victory." This depiction of the war was the reiteration of what Nasrallah's master, the supreme leader in Iran, Ali Khamenei, had said. The latter, in a message to Nasrallah on August 14, 2006, stated that the war was "a divine victory for Islam."

THE INTERNATIONAL SPECIAL TRIBUNAL FOR LEBANON

Just two days before the cabinet headed by Prime Minister Fouad Siniora was to approve the blueprint for the internationally established Special Tribunal for Lebanon, the Shi'ite ministers in the cabinet representing Hezbollah and Amal resigned. Nevertheless, Siniora convened a cabinet meeting attended by eighteen members on November 13, 2006, during which the blueprint of the international Special Tribunal for Lebanon was approved. The issue of the tribunal was and still is a matter that affects Syria and Hezbollah that were responsible for the assassination of former Prime Minister Rafic Hariri and all other terrorist operations. After a visit to Syria and Iran, the speaker of the Lebanese parliament, Nabih Berri, began depicting the cabinet led by Prime Minister Siniora as illegitimate and unconstitutional. Berri had also refused to accept a petition signed by the majority of members of parliament (70 out of a total of 128) to convene a parliamentary session to discuss and vote on the statute of the Special Tribunal for

29

Lebanon that was approved by the Siniora cabinet. According to Walid Jumblatt, Berri had been threatened by Syria and Iran as though "there is a gun pointed to his [Berri's] head." The strategy of Hezbollah and its two partners was to question the "legitimacy" of the Siniora cabinet. First, a prominent member of the Lebanese cabinet and a leading critic of Syria and Hezbollah, Pierre Gemayel, was assassinated on November 21, 2006. He was a charismatic scion of the Gemayel family, son of a former president, and he had struck up a close friendship with Saad Hariri. Second, Hezbollah and its allies began a permanent sit-in on December 1, 2006, close to Prime Minister Fouad Siniora's official residence in downtown Beirut, forcing the closing down of hundreds of shops and businesses, further adding to unemployment and the economic downturn of the country.

Hezbollah's leader, Nasrallah, was not concerned about the consequences of his action because Hezbollah had an independent source of income from Iran. Contrary to all democratic traditions, and unprecedented in Lebanon, the speaker of the House, Nabih Berri, closed down parliament for fourteen months from March 2007 until May 2008. There were two reasons for that. The first reason was to prevent parliamentary endorsement of the Special Tribunal for Lebanon; however, this ironically led to the passing of the United Nations Security Council Resolution 1757 on May 30, 2007, setting up the international Special Tribunal for Lebanon under Chapter VII, which made its rulings binding and granted it the powers to interrogate and indict officials who otherwise would have remained unaccountable. The second reason was that after September 25, 2007, if the parliament were to be convened, the Cedar Revolution majority could elect a new president of Lebanon to succeed President Émile Lahoud, whose tenure was set to expire on November 23, 2007. Therefore Parliament was kept closed by the Speaker of the House to prevent such an eventuality from happening.

A GROWING OPPOSITION TO HEZBOLLAH AND AMAL IN THE SHI'ITE COMMUNITY

Walid Jumblatt, the Druze leader, had persuasively asserted that Hezbollah's leader Hassan

Nasrallah "is not Lebanese because he receives his orders from the Syrian regime and the [Islamic] Republic of Iran." If Nasrallah were Lebanese, Jumblatt added, he would have accepted being under the auspices of the Lebanese legitimate authorities, and not keep "his own state, his own weapons, his own public, his own finances and his own economy." According to Jumblatt, Nasrallah has his own culture, "which totally differs from our culture; it is the culture of martyrdom which in the final analysis means the culture of sorrow, misery and death, and is not like our culture of love, hope and life." To counter what Hezbollah and its two masters had done to the Shi'ite community in Lebanon, a group of clergymen and scions of leading Shi'ite families met on July 13, 2007, in Beirut, and founded what was called "The Gathering of Those Committed to Lebanon." In their declaration, the founders stated: "We are aware that to move away from the path of development and modernity would abolish Lebanon." They added: "We want to break the monopoly of representation that Hezbollah and Amal exercise within the Shi'ite community . . . we want the establishment of a modern democratic civil state . . . a state where belonging to Lebanon is the only option . . . a state that will be able to assert its authority and sovereignty over all its territories, and will have the sole right to carry arms and to make the decision about war and peace." An article by the Shi'ite journalist Ahmad Ayyash published in the *al-Nahar* newspaper in October 2011 stated that change will reach the Shi'ite community because the present leaders of Hezbollah and Amal, Hassan Nasrallah and Nabih Berri represent "the tyrants of Damascus and Tehran," and as "a new dawn in Syria" is not far away, it is inevitable that the present dominant leaders of the Shi'ite community will be swept away with the wind of change that is blowing from the Arab world.

THE LEBANESE ARMY DEFEATS THE TERRORIST ORGANIZATION FATAH AL-ISLAM

The leader of Fatah al-Islam was Shaker al-Abssi, a Jordanian of Palestinian origins who was sentenced to death in Jordan in 2004 for his role in

33

the murder of the American diplomat Laurence Foley in Amman, Jordan, on October 28, 2002. Abssi fled to Syria and in 2005 he was sent to the Palestinian camps of Hulwah and Qusaya in the Biqa' region of Lebanon, located close to the Syrian border. According to Walid Jumblatt, Fatah al-Islam was nothing but an instrument of the Syrian regime under the sway of Syrian intelligence. Fatah al-Islam had entrenched itself in the Nahr al-Bared Palestinian camp in northern Lebanon, and it took the Lebanese army 160 days (from May 20 until September 2, 2007) of fierce fighting to defeat this terrorist organization. One hundred and sixty-three soldiers and officers died in this war that reasserted the strong national identity of the Lebanese, as the fallen members of the Lebanese army were Sunnis, Christians, Druze, and Shi'ites. The commander of the Lebanese army, General Michel Suleiman, became the most popular figure in Lebanon.

On September 2, 2007, when the Lebanese army declared victory over Fatah al-Islam, there were spontaneous celebrations all over the country. The army brigades that liberated Nahr al-Bared camp made their journey of 100 kilometers from the camp to Beirut on September 4, 2007, and were welcomed by thousands of Lebanese who had strewn their path with rice and roses. Music, patriotic songs, dances, and fireworks accompanied the returning army units throughout their journey. The only detractors were the pro-Syrian and pro-Iranian groups like Hezbollah, whose leader had expressed strong reservations about using the Lebanese army to enter Nahr al-Bared to defeat Fatah al-Islam. The joy that accompanied the triumph of the Lebanese army was not destined to last, as it was followed by the assassination, on December 12, 2007, of the director of military operations in the Lebanese army, Brigadier General François al-Hajj, who was instrumental in defeating Fatah al-Islam. His funeral on December 15, 2007, was another occasion for the Lebanese people, despite the stormy and rainy weather, to express support for the Lebanese army as his funeral procession traveled from Beirut to his hometown close to Lebanese-Israeli border.

HEZBOLLAH USES FORCE AGAINST SAAD AL-HARIRI AND
WALID JUMBLATT IN BEIRUT AND MOUNT LEBANON

It was discovered in April 2008 that Iran and Hezbollah took advantage of the rebuilding of the roads and bridges that were destroyed in the war of 2006 that Hezbollah had provoked, to install fiber-optic lines of communication throughout Lebanon. In a meeting with the U.S. chargé d'affaires in Beirut, the Lebanese minister of telecommunications, Marwan Hamadeh, revealed the existence of a fiber-optic network that he had illustrated with a map showing "lines running from Beirut, around both sides of the airport, into the south below the Litani [river] and back up through the Bekaa Valley to the far north." The first words uttered by Hamadeh to the chargé d'affaires were "the Iran Telecom is taking over the country!" Hamadeh pointed out that Iran had used the Iranian Fund for the Reconstruction of Lebanon to create its outpost on the Mediterranean. This was not new, as Walid Jumblatt had argued that when Iranian President Mahmoud Ahmadinejad had claimed that Iran and Lebanon constituted "one body," this was tantamount to an indirect merger of Lebanon into "the Persian Empire."

The Lebanese cabinet decided on May 5, 2008, to dismiss the head of security at Beirut International Airport because he had allowed Hezbollah to install cameras to spy on passengers using the airport. The Lebanese cabinet also declared that the fiber-optic network installed by Hezbollah all over the country was illegal. These decisions were used by Hezabollah and its allies to wage a war starting on May 7, 2008, against the Sunni quarters of Beirut by occupying and closing down all the media outlets (TV, newspaper, radio) of the Future Movement headed by Saad Hariri. Simultaneously Hezbollah waged a war against Jumblatt's Druze regions in Aley and in al-Shouf in Mount Lebanon. The five days of fighting resulted in over eighty deaths and several hundred people wounded. The Lebanese army intervened on May 13, 2008, to prevent escalation of the conflict. Nevertheless, by using force, Hezbollah and its allies triumphed over the Cedar Revolution leaders because on May 14, 2008, the Lebanese cabinet had to rescind the decisions made on May 5, 2008. Thus, neither the chief security officer at the Beirut International Airport was removed from his post, nor was Hezbollah's fiber-optic network dismantled. Hezbollah resorted to force for another long-standing demand, to have one-third plus one seat in the Lebanese cabinet. According to the Lebanese constitution, all major decisions by the cabinet need a two-thirds majority. So, by having one-third plus one seat in the cabinet, Hezbollah and its allies will be able to veto all major decisions that they oppose.

The ruler of Qatar, Emir Hamad bin Khalifa al-Thani, had stepped in as a mediator in the Lebanese crisis by inviting the fourteen leaders of all the major political parties and parliamentary blocs in Lebanon to attend a dialogue conference in Qatar's capital, Doha. After five days of discussions, an accord was reached on May 21, 2008, that specified the election of the popular commander of the Lebanese army General Michel Suleiman as president of Lebanon. Parliament, which had been shut down by its pro-Syrian speaker Nabih Berri for fourteen months, was reopened on May 25, 2008, to elect Suleiman as president with a vast majority of 118 votes out of a total of 127. The accord reached in Doha also gave the pro-Syrian opposition one-third plus one seat in the Lebanese cabinet (eleven out of thirty). In this respect, the accord reached in Doha had undermined the Consociational Democracy that characterized Lebanon from 1943 until 1972. The political scientist Arend Lijphart coined the term Consociational Democracy, which he used to describe Lebanon as well as similar countries like Switzerland. In Lebanon, Consociational Democracy meant that all the major religious sects should be represented in the Lebanese cabinet, but will be selected from the majority that had won the parliamentary elections. By using force in May 2008, Hezbollah and its allies had managed, through the accord reached in Doha on May 21, 2008, to impose the one-third-plus-one representation of the opposition (that is, the minority in Parliament) in the Lebanese cabinet, along with veto power and the ability to force the resignation of the whole cabinet. Despite the undemocratic feature of such an arrangement, Prime Minister Fouad Siniora depicted the cabinet that he formed on July 11, 2008, after forty-five days of consultations, as a government of "national unity."

THE PARLIAMENTARY ELECTIONS OF JUNE 2009 AND THE SAAD AL-HARIRI CABINET

On June 7, 2009, parliamentary elections took place all over Lebanon, which led to the victory of the Cedar Revolution coalition with 71 seats out of a total 128. Despite that, it took Saad Hariri, who was asked by President Suleiman to form a new cabinet, 135 days of consultations and negotiations to complete the task. In this new cabinet, Hezbollah and its allies were given again the one-third plus one seat (eleven out of the total thirty), and the ability to veto all major decisions and even to force the resignation of the whole cabinet.

As the indictments by the Special Tribunal for Lebanon of those responsible for killing former Prime Minister Rafic Hariri were on the verge of being issued, Hezbollah and the other pro-Syrian members of the cabinet asked Prime Minister Saad Hariri to convene a meeting to discuss how to sever Lebanon's relations with the Special Tribunal for Lebanon. However, Hariri refused to do so. On January 12, 2011, while Saad Hariri was meeting President Obama in the White House, the eleven pro-Syrian members of the Lebanese cabinet resigned, forcing the resignation of the whole cabinet. It was expected that the leader of the majority in Parliament, Saad Hariri, would be asked again to form a new cabinet; however, Hezbollah preempted by sending its militiamen, clad in black shirts, to the streets of Beirut, threatening Walid Jumblatt that his Druze mountain strongholds would be attacked again, as had happened in May 2008. Consequently most of Jumblatt's parliamentary bloc shifted to the pro-Syrian side, allowing Najib Mikati, a Sunni tycoon from Tripoli and close friend of President Assad, to be designated, on January 25, 2011, as the new prime minister.

In response to what happened, the resentment against Hezbollah's domination of Lebanon rose by leaps and bounds. This resentment was manifested when the rally on the sixth anniversary of March 14, 2005, was held on Sunday

March 13, 2011, attended by a vast number of people, second only to the original rally of 2005. Christians, Sunnis Druze, and Shi'ites chanted against the arms kept by Hezbollah. Their slogan was "No to the domination of the arms [of Hezbollah], yes to the Lebanese army."

THE INDICTMENT OF LEADING HEZBOLLAH MEMBERS IN THE ASSASSINATION OF FORMER PRIME MINISTER RAFIC HARIRI

On June 30, 2011, the Special Tribunal for Lebanon indicted four members of Hezbollah, and on August 17, 2011, it provided biographical information on the four suspects and a forty-seven-page indictment. The conspiracy to assassinate Rafic Hariri was headed by Mustafa Badr al-Din, a high-ranking Hezbollah official, who was formerly jailed in Kuwait for bombing the U.S. and French Embassies in Kuwait on December 12, 1983. The other senior official of Hezbollah, Salim Ayyash, was in charge of the operation on the ground. Warrants issued by the Special Tribunal were sent to the Lebanese state prosecutor to find and arrest the indicted individuals within thirty days. The leader of Hezbollah, Hassan Nasrallah, in a televised speech on July 2, 2011, referred to the four indicted members of his party as "honorable brothers." He declared, defiantly, that "they cannot find them in 30 days or 60 days, or in one year or two years, in 30 years or 300 years." Nasrallah accused the implausible other, Israel, of the assassination of Rafic Hariri. No one could take seriously such an accusation, as it belongs to bygone times. It shows how out of touch the leader of Hezbollah is with Lebanese public opinion.

Saad Hariri, who had stayed abroad since the fall of his cabinet, blamed Syrian President Assad and Nasrallah for his ouster from power by undemocratic means. He welcomed the decision by the Special Tribunal for Lebanon to indict members of Hezbollah, saying it is "the first time in the history of the Arab world that there is a tribunal to put on trial those who killed politicians."

43

THE REVOLUTION IN SYRIA

President Bashar Assad was confident that the Arab Spring that began in Lebanon in March 2005—and which gained momentum more than five years later, with revolutions spreading to Tunisia, Egypt, Libya, and Yemen—would not affect Syria. On March 15, 2011, contrary to his prediction, a revolution erupted in Syria, starting with the southern city of Dir'a and quickly spreading to the central and north central cities of Homs, Rastan, and Hama, as well as Idlib, Jisr al-Shagur, Ma'arrat al-Numan, and eventually all over Syria, including Damascus and the commercial city of Aleppo. It began as a peaceful, nonviolent revolution, with protestors seeking "freedom and human dignity." The peaceful phase of the revolution was brief, and as the military crackdown by the Assad regime began in earnest, it led to armed resistance by the opposition with the formation of the Free Syrian Army composed of army defectors and volunteers. Increasingly, non-Syrian jihadists were to join the war, depicting the Assad regime as heretical and ungodly. President Assad has used his full military arsenal, including artillery, tanks, helicopters, and military jets against the popular revolution, but he was unable to contain it, let alone end it. As of this writing, the number of people killed in this crackdown has reached 70,000, and the authorities have detained tens of thousands of people. The Assad regimes, whether that of the father or the son, have been characterized by ruthlessness. It was Rifaat al-Assad who said on July 1, 1980, when he was the henchman for his brother President Hafez Assad, that he was willing to kill one million Syrians if necessary to keep the Assad regime in power.

IRAN AND HEZBOLLAH ARE ACTIVELY SUPPORTING THE AL-ASSAD REGIME

Syria's allies, Hezbollah and the Iranian regime, have joined in the war against the Syrian opposition. Thousands of Iranian Revolutionary Guard Corps have been fighting in Syria. Similarly, thousands of Hezbollah fighters have been involved in combat in Damascus and especially in the province of Homs, contiguous to the northern east region of Lebanon where Hezbollah has a major stronghold. Over a hundred Hezbollah fighters have been killed in Syria, and they have been buried discreetly in their hometowns in Lebanon without mentioning where their deaths had occurred. Only when a high-ranking commander of Hezbollah was killed in Syria was there a public funeral, taking place on August 10, 2012. The death of a Hezbollah fighter killed in Syria is explained as occurring "while performing his jihadi duty." The highest-ranking Hezbollah commander in charge of military operations in Syria, Ali Hussein Nassif, was killed on September 29, 2012, and was buried in his native village with a public funeral procession attended by high-ranking Hezbollah officials in the Biqa' region.

In addition to the thousands of fighters provided by Iran and Hezbollah to Syria, Iran has supplied President Assad with over $10 billion to prop up his regime. Both Iran and Hezbollah are concerned about what will happen if Assad were to be toppled. The future of that alliance is at stake.

PRESIDENT AL-ASSAD CONTINUES HIS
TERRORIST WAR ON LEBANON

After a tip from the head of a private security firm, the Internal Security Forces raided, on August 9, 2012, former cabinet member Michel Samaha's house and arrested him on charges of transporting from Syria twenty-four explosive devices meant to be used in terrorist attacks in the northern region of Akkar to foment conflict between Sunnis and Christians. Samaha was a close adviser to President Assad. The evidence found was incriminating, with a video that was secretly recorded in which Samaha asserts that the planting of explosives is what President Assad wants. The overwhelming evidence prompted the military court judge to issue a summons for Brigadier General Ali Mamlouk, who heads the Syrian National Security Bureau and supervises all security agencies, and who reports directly to President Assad. The Syrian response to uncovering the terrorist plot that involved Michel Samaha and his Syrian masters was to assassinate the head of the Information Branch of the Internal Security Forces, Major

General Wissam al-Hassan, on October 19, 2012, as he was leaving his residence in the Ashrafiya quarter of Beirut for his office. Hassan was in charge of the branch in the Internal Security Forces that deciphered the data that led to the indictment of leading members of Hezbollah in the assassination of the former prime minister, Rafic Hariri. Lebanese President Michel Suleiman gave a speech at Wissam al-Hassan's funeral, stating that "this assassination was directed against the Lebanese state." Suleiman called also for the judiciary to hasten the investigation of Michel Samaha's case and to issue the indictment as soon as possible. The leaders of the Cedar Revolution called for a peaceful, nonviolent boycott of the Lebanese cabinet of Prime Minister Najib Mikati that is controlled by Syria, Iran, and Hezbollah and that serves their interests "at the expense of the interests of Lebanon, its people and its security."

CONCLUSION

Lebanon has been subjected to the onslaught of Syria, Iran, and Hezbollah for three decades.

The first two attempts to reestablish a Lebanese polity imbued with the free, liberal, democratic, and pluralistic ideals were nipped in the bud by President Hafez al-Assad, when he killed President-elect Bachir Gemayel on September 14, 1982, and then dislodged from power the interim prime minister, General Michel Aoun, on October 13, 1990. If the Maronite Catholic political leaders led the first two attempts, the third attempt that culminated in the Cedar Revolution on March 14, 2005, had begun in September 2000 by the Maronite Catholic Church and its Patriarch Sfair. At present the ideals of the Cedar Revolution, supported by the majority of the Lebanese people, constitute a glimmer of hope for Lebanon to remain free, pluralistic, and open to the whole world.

The unraveling of the Iran-Syria-Hezbollah axis is in the offing, as the Syrian ruler will never be able to reestablish his authority over all of the country. His inevitable departure from Damascus could lead to his retreat into the Alawite region in northwestern Syria, bordered by Turkey, Lebanon, and the Mediterranean. Perhaps the old dream of the Alawites of forming their own state might yet come true. After all, the grandfather of the Syrian president had signed a petition, dated June 15, 1936, with other notables of the Alawite community addressed to the French Prime Minister Léon Blum, asking for an independent Alawite state. The question is whether the new rulers in Damascus would accept a Syria that will be landlocked. Can Turkey accept the establishment of an Alawite state in Syria, when it has 20 million Alawites of its own?

A PERSONAL NOTE

To talk about Lebanon as free, liberal, democratic, and open to the world reminds me of the Lebanon that I knew in my childhood and youth during the period 1950 to 1965. I was fortunate enough to live in Beirut during that golden age. My sister and I went to an elementary school, adjacent to the Jewish quarter of Wadi Abu Jamil, run by a Quaker headmistress. A couple of hundred meters away, the presidential residence was located on Qantari Street. Schools were all over the place. If one went up the hill, there were the St. Joseph's School run by nuns and the British School, among many others. If one went toward downtown following the tramway, there were the Jewish Alliance School and the Besancon School.

Although it was a golden age, it was marred by a brief civil war that lasted one hundred days, beginning in May 1958. As a consequence of that, my family moved to the Ras Beirut quarter, that is, the tip of the peninsula where the sea surrounds Beirut on three sides. Sitting on the balcony of our apartment I could see and smell the Mediterranean. It was a paradise on earth with cafés, restaurants, shops, bookstores, cinemas, and beaches. There was also the lovely campus of the American University of Beirut. All these places were walking distance from where we lived. This was the cosmopolitan Beirut, with a large number of Americans and Europeans along with Lebanese of all backgrounds. My family and I felt totally at home in Ras Beirut.

The Lebanon that I knew was not just Beirut and the Mediterranean coast. As the poet, essayist, and statesman Michel Chiha put it: "Lebanon is the interpenetration of the Mountain and the Sea." By virtue of his profession as the headmaster of a prominent school in Beirut, my father had long summer holidays and he liked to spend them in the mountains of Lebanon. My father belonged to a Greek Orthodox family from the town of al-Khiyam in the Marjeyoun (meaning the meadow of springs) region of southern Lebanon. I was delighted to spend the summers there, savoring my favorite fruits of grapes and figs, visiting our land in the Marj, and drinking the cold and pristine water of the holy spring of Derdarah. It was there that I heard from my grandmother the legendary stories about my grandfather who had forged political alliances and links with the Druze notable family of Qays in the nearby town of Hasbaya, with the feudal lord Kamel al-Asaad of Taibay and with the notable Abdallah family of his hometown al-Khiyam.

What was striking at that time was the peace and tranquility that characterized Lebanon. Whether in Marjeyoun close to the Israeli border or in the mountains of Keserwan where my family had also spent summer holidays, peace and security prevailed. I can recall driving up to

Rayfoun, when at that time the Lebanese president, Fouad Chehab, had a summer residence on the way in the town of Ajaltoun. A couple of times we were driving behind the president, who was sitting in the back with his driver in front and the only security guard was just one soldier riding on a motorcycle!

Nevertheless, Lebanon was not a perfect country. It had its feuds and follies, its sectarian faultlines. Almost none could foresee the ruin that would befall it in the decades to come. A nemesis overtook its civility, and two more powerful states, Iran and Syria, unleashed on that fragile land their brand of politics—mayhem and unlimited violence. The small country once celebrated for beauty and splendor came to stand for endless wars perpetuated by external powers. The Lebanese had been helpless to hold their own against those who undid the peace of their country. Worse yet, in the ascendency of Hezbollah, some Lebanese themselves had aided and abetted the forces of destruction.

BIBLIOGRAPHICAL ESSAY

Introduction

Hafez al-Assad's alliance with Iran was not affected by the Iran-Iraq war of 1980–1988, even though Syria shared with Iraq the language and the Pan-Arab Nationalism of the Ba'th. This had clearly shown the triumph of religion over ideology. See Marius Deeb, "Syria and the War on Iraq," in *Regime Change in Iraq: The Transatlantic and Regional Dimensions*, edited by Christian-Peter Hanelt et al., Florence, Italy, Robert Schuman Centre for Advanced Studies, 2004, pp. 143–53.

For the formation of Hezbollah, see Marius Deeb, *Militant Islamic Movements in Lebanon: Origins, Social Basis and Ideology*, Washington, D.C., Center for Contemporary Arab Studies, 1986, pp. 13–22. See also Marius Deeb, *Syria's Terrorist War on Lebanon and the Peace Process*, New York, Palgrave Macmillan, 2003, pp. 81–82.

For the massacre of civilians in the Sabra and Shatila Palestinian camps, see the revisionist explanation of putting the onus on Syria. Franck Salameh, "Revisiting a Massacre in Lebanon's Civil War—Were Lebanese Christians

Responsible?" George Mason University's History News Network, December 5, 2011.

Both scholars and policymakers overlooked the paramount importance of the Golan Heights disengagement agreement between Syria and Israel, signed on May 31, 1974. Hafez al-Assad told Henry Kissinger: "What is it the Israelis want? I already agreed that we won't touch any settlements.... The basic thing the Israelis ought to understand is that if we get a satisfactory settlement in disengagement [the Golan Heights agreement], then we can have a long stamina there, then we can stay there and settle and reconstruct." See Henry Kisssinger, *Years of Upheaval*, Boston and Toronto, Little, Brown and Company, 1982, pp. 1082–83. This reveals that President Assad was not interested in recovering the Israeli-occupied Golan Heights.

Terrorism and Hostage Taking
For the terrorist operations in the 1980s, see Marius Deeb, *Syria's Terrorist War on Lebanon and the Peace Process*, pp. 78–181.

For more than the symbolic importance of the assassination of the president of the American University of Beirut, Malcolm Kerr, see Fouad Ajami, *The Dream Palace of the Arabs: A Generation's Odyssey*, New York, Pantheon Books, 1998, pp. 100–09.

For hostage taking and how it was used by Syria and Iran to achieve their objectives, see Marius Deeb, "More

Than Meets the Eye," *The World and I*, Vol. 5, No, 7, July 1990, pp. 60–67. See also Marius Deeb, *Syria's Terrorist War on Lebanon and the Peace Process*, passim.

For Michel Aoun's popularity while defying Syria, see Carole Dagher, *Les Paris du General*, Beirut, La Seil Press, 1992.

For showing that Syria had no intention of making peace with Israel, and for the wars that Hezbollah had provoked to undermine the peace process, see Marius Deeb, *Syria's Terrorist War on Lebanon and the Peace Process*, pp. 183–211.

Patriarch Sfair: The Conscience of Lebanon
The prestigious *Al-Nahar* newspaper had covered the memorandum issued by Patriarch Sfair in September 2000, and his journey to the southern part of Mount Lebanon in early August 2001 that led to the reconciliation between the Druze and Maronite communities.

The Anti-Syrian Opposition Movement Gathers Strength
Other than *Al-Nahar* newspaper, there is the short monograph in Arabic entitled *Al-Rafiq al-Sahir* by Fares Khashan, a prominent journalist who was close to former Prime Minister Rafic Hariri. For the reasons for Syria's assassination of Prime Minister Rashid Karami, see Marius Deeb, *Syria's Terrorist War on Lebanon and the Peace Process*, pp. 136–38. For the crucial role played by the

Christians and the Druze immediately after the assassination of Rafic Hariri, see the article by the journalist Michael Young, "The General Out of His Labyrinth," *The Daily Star*, June 14, 2005.

The Cedar Revolution

For the most extensive coverage of the unprecedented Cedar Revolution of March 14, 2005, and the events that followed, see *Al-Nahar* newspaper. For showing that the 2005 parliamentary elections were not free and fair in regions controlled by Hezbollah and Amal, see the article by Fadi Tawfiq and Luqman Salim "Al-Janub: Kayf Intikhabat Hurrah fi Dar al-Harb?" *Al-Nahar*, June 20, 2005.

The Unholy Alliance Versus the Cedar Revolution

For the terrorism unleashed by the "unholy alliance" against the Cedar Revolution and for the clash between the two cultures, see the extensive coverage by *Al-Nahar* newspaper.

Hezbollah Provokes a War with Israel

For the most extensive coverage of this devastating war, see *Al-Nahar* newspaper.

The International Special Tribunal for Lebanon

For the establishment of the Special Tribunal for Lebanon, the assassination of the cabinet minister Pierre Gemayel, the Hezbollah permanent sit-in in downtown Beirut that lasted eighteenth months, and the closing down of Parliament by the Amal leader Nabih Berri that lasted for fourteen months, see the extensive coverage in *Al-Nahar* newspaper.

A Growing Opposition to Hezbollah and Amal in the Shi'ite Community

For opposition to Hezbollah and Amal within the Sh'ite community, see the coverage by *Al-Nahar* newspaper. See also the article by Ahmad Ayyash, "Wa al-Shi'ah fi Lubnan Yuridun," *Al-Nahar*, October 15, 2011.

The Lebanese Army Defeats the Terrorist Organization Fatah al-Islam

For the battle against Fatah al-Islam and the celebration following its defeat, see the full coverage by *Al-Nahar* newspaper.

Hezbollah Uses Force against Saad al-Hariri and Walid Jumblatt in Beirut and Mount Lebanon

For the fiber-optic system installed by Hezbollah, see the classified cable, released by Wikileaks, from the U.S. chargé d'affaires, Michele Sison, dated April 8, 2008. For Hezbollah's war against al-Hariri and Jumblatt, see the full coverage by *Al-Nahar* newspaper.

The Parliamentary Elections of June 2009 and the Saad al-Hariri Cabinet

For the events that led to the fall of al-Hariri's cabinet, and for the mass rally on the sixth anniversary of March 14, 2005, see the full coverage in *Al-Nahar* newspaper.

The Indictment of Leading Hezbollah Members in the Assassination of Former Prime Minister Rafic Hariri

For the text of the indictment of leading members of Hezbollah and the reaction of the leader of Hezbollah, see the full coverage in *Al-Nahar* newspaper.

The Revolution in Syria

For the early phases of the revolution in Syria, see the excellent coverage and analysis by Fouad Ajami, *The Syrian Rebellion*, Stanford, California, Hoover Institution Press, 2012, pp. 69–194.

For the threat by Rifaat al-Assad in 1980 that he was ready to sacrifice one million Syrians to keep the regime in power, see Michel Seurat, writing under the name Gerard Michaud, "The Importance of Bodyguards," in *MERIP REPORTS: Middle East Research and Information Project*, vol. XII, no. 9, November–December 1982.

Iran and Hezbollah Are Actively Supporting the al-Assad Regime

For the active role played by Iran and Hezbollah in support of the Syrian president, al-Assad, see *Al-Nahar* and *Al-Mustaqbal* newspapers.

President al-Assad Continues His Terrorist War on Lebanon

For uncovering the Syrian terrorist plot using former cabinet minister Michel Samaha and the assassination of Wissam al-Hassan, see the coverage by *Al-Nahar* and *Al-Mustaqbal* newspapers.

About the Author

Marius Deeb who has a doctorate from Oxford University is a leading authority on Middle Eastern Politics and History. Professor Deeb teaches at the School of Advanced International Studies of John Hopkins University. He had previously taught at Indiana University, American University of Beirut, and Georgetown University. His publications include *Party Politics in Egypt: The Wafd and Its Rivals, 1919–1939, The Lebanese Civil War, Libya Since Revolution: Aspects of Social and Political Development* (co-authored with Mary-Jane Deeb), *Militant Islamic Movements in Lebanon: Origins, Social Basis and Ideology,* and *Syria's Terrorist War on Lebanon and the Peace Process.* Professor Deeb's research interests include the study of political parties and movements, militant Islam in all its varieties, the Christian communities of the Middle East and Islam and the West.

HERBERT AND JANE DWIGHT
WORKING GROUP ON
ISLAMISM AND THE
INTERNATIONAL ORDER

THE HERBERT AND JANE DWIGHT WORKING GROUP ON ISLAMISM AND THE INTERNATIONAL ORDER seeks to engage in the task of reversing Islamic radicalism through reforming and strengthening the legitimate role of the state across the entire Muslim world. Efforts will draw on the intellectual resources of an array of scholars and practitioners from within the United States and abroad, to foster the pursuit of modernity, human flourishing, and the rule of law and reason in Islamic lands—developments that are critical to the very order of the international system.

The Working Group is co-chaired by Hoover fellows Fouad Ajami and Charles Hill, with an active participation by Hoover Institution Director John Raisian. Current core membership includes Russell A. Berman, Abbas Milani, and Shelby Steele, with contributions from Zeyno Baran, Reuel Marc Gerecht, Ziad Haider, R. John Hughes, Nibras Kazimi, Bernard Lewis, Habib Malik, Camille Pecastaing, Lieutenant Colonel Joel Rayburn, and Joshua Teitelbaum.

INDEX